Poems
to read to
the very young

Selected by Josette Frank
Illustrated by Eloise Wilkin

RANDOM HOUSE 🏠 NEW YORK

Library of Congress Cataloging in Publication Data: Main entry under title: Poems to read to the very young. Includes
index. SUMMARY: A collection of short poems on various subjects, by Robert Louis Stevenson, A. A. Milne, Christina
Rossetti, and other authors.   1. Children's poetry, English.   2. Children's poetry, American.   [1. English poetry—
Collections. 2. American poetry—Collections]   I. Frank, Josette [date].   II. Wilkin, Eloise Burns, ill.
PR1195.C47P6   82-518   AACR2   ISBN: 0-394-85188-9 (trade);   0-394-95188-3 (lib. bdg.)

Manufactured in the United States of America   0

Poetry credits appear on page 45.

Good-Morning

One day I saw a downy duck,
With feathers on his back;
I said, "Good-morning, downy duck,"
And he said, "Quack, quack, quack."

One day I saw a timid mouse,
He was so shy and meek;
I said, "Good-morning, timid mouse,"
And he said,
                "Squeak,
                        squeak,
                                squeak."

One day I saw a curly dog,
I met him with a bow;
I said, "Good-morning, curly dog,"
And he said, "Bow-wow-wow."

One day I saw a scarlet bird,
He woke me from my sleep;
I said, "Good-morning, scarlet bird,"
And he said,
                "Cheep,
                        cheep,
                                cheep."

—Muriel Sipe

Time to Rise

A birdie with a yellow bill
Hopped upon the window sill,
Cocked his shining eye and said:
"Ain't you 'shamed, you sleepy-head!"

—Robert Louis Stevenson

Merry Sunshine

"Good morning, Merry Sunshine,
    How did you wake so soon,
You've scared the little stars away
    And shined away the moon.
I saw you go to sleep last night
    Before I ceased my playing;
How did you get 'way over there?
    And where have you been staying?"

"I never go to sleep, dear child,
    I just go round to see
My little children of the East,
    Who rise and watch for me.
I waken all the birds and bees
    And flowers on my way,
And now come back to see the child
    Who stayed out late at play."

—Anonymous

Singing–Time

I wake in the morning early
And always, the very first thing,
I poke out my head and I sit up in bed
And I sing and I sing and I sing.

—Rose Fyleman

Susan Blue

Oh, Susan Blue,
How do you do?
Please may I go for a walk with you?
Where shall we go:
Oh, I know—
Down in the meadow where the cowslips grow!

—Kate Greenaway

The Cow

The friendly cow all red and white
   I love with all my heart;
She gives me cream with all her might
   To eat with apple-tart.

She wanders lowing here and there
   And yet she cannot stray,
All in the pleasant open air,
   The pleasant light of day;

And blown by all the winds that pass
   And wet with all the showers,
She walks among the meadow grass
   And eats the meadow flowers.

—Robert Louis Stevenson

Spring

Sound the flute!
Now it's mute.
Birds delight
Day and Night;
Nightingale
In the dale,
Lark in Sky,
Merrily,
Merrily, merrily, to welcome in the Year.

Little Boy,
Full of joy;
Little Girl,
Sweet and small;
Cock does crow,
So do you;
Merry voice,
Infant noise,
Merrily, merrily, to welcome in the Year.

Little Lamb
Here I am;
Come and lick
My white neck;
Let me pull
Your soft Wool;
Let me kiss
Your soft face;
Merrily, merrily, welcome in the Year.

—William Blake

9

Field Mouse to Kitchen Mouse

I live upon seeds of grasses
    And raspberries chill with dew,
And fallen acorns and hickory nuts
    And little green apples, too.

Oh, doesn't your cheese taste musty and old,
    And don't your crumbs taste dry,
Which you have to nibble under a roof
    And never under the sky?

—Elizabeth Coatsworth

The Rabbit Skip

Hop Skip Jump
A rabbit won't bite.

Hop Skip Jump
A rabbit won't fight.

Hop Skip Jump
A rabbit runs light.

Hop Skip Jump
He's out of sight.

—Margaret Wise Brown

Mr. Rabbit

Mr. Rabbit has a habit
That is very cute to see.

He wrinkles up and crinkles up
His little nose at me.

I like my little rabbit,
And I like his little brother.

And we have a lot of fun
Making faces at each other.

—Dixie Willson

Once I Saw a Little Bird

Once I saw a little bird
Come hop, hop, hop;
So I cried, "Little bird,
Will you stop, stop, stop?"

And was going to the window,
To say, "How do you do?"
But he shook his little tail
And far away he flew.

—Old Nursery Rhyme

Some One

Some one came knocking
  At my wee, small door;
Some one came knocking,
  I'm sure—sure—sure;
I listened, I opened,
  I looked to left and right,
But nought there was a-stirring
  In the still dark night.
Only the busy beetle
  Tap-tapping in the wall,
Only from the forest
  The screech-owl's call,
Only the cricket whistling
  While the dewdrops fall,
So I know not who came knocking,
  At all, at all, at all.

—Walter de la Mare

Bird Talk

"Think . . ." said the robin,
"Think . . ." said the jay,
sitting in the garden,
talking one day.

"Think about people—
the way they grow:
they don't have feathers
at all, you know.

"They don't eat beetles,
they don't grow wings,
they don't like sitting
on wires and things.

"Think!" said the robin.
"Think!" said the jay.
"Aren't people funny
to be that way?"

—Aileen Fisher

11

Puppy and I

I met a man as I went walking;
We got talking,
Man and I.
"Where are you going to, Man?" I said
(I said to the Man as he went by).
"Down to the village, to get some bread.
Will you come with me?" "No, not I."

I met a Horse as I went walking;
We got talking,
Horse and I.
"Where are you going to, Horse, today?"
(I said to the Horse as he went by).
"Down to the village to get some hay.
Will you come with me?" "No, not I."

I met a Woman as I went walking;
We got talking,
Woman and I.
"Where are you going to, Woman, so early?"
(I said to the Woman as she went by).
"Down to the village to get some barley.
Will you come with me?" "No, not I."

I met some Rabbits as I went walking;
We got talking,
Rabbits and I.
"Where are you going in your brown fur coats?"
(I said to the Rabbits as they went by).
"Down to the village to get some oats.
Will you come with us?" "No, not I."

I met a Puppy as I went walking;
We got talking,
Puppy and I.
"Where are you going this nice fine day?"
(I said to the Puppy as he went by).
"Up in the hills to roll and play."
"*I'll* come with you, Puppy," said I.

—A. A. Milne

The Birthday Child

Everything's been different
    All the day long,
Lovely things have happened,
    Nothing has gone wrong.

Nobody has scolded me,
    Everyone has smiled.
Isn't it delicious
    To be a birthday child?

        —Rose Fyleman

Five Years Old

Please, everybody, look at me!
Today I'm five years old, you see!
And after this, I won't be four,
Not ever, ever, any more!
I won't be three—or two—or one.
For that was when I'd first begun.
Now I'll be five a while, and then
I'll soon be something else again!

        —Mary Louise Allen

Little Black Bug

Little black bug,
Little black bug,
Where have you been?
I've been under the rug.
Said little black bug.

Little green fly,
Little green fly,
Where have you been?
I've been way up high,
Said little green fly.
Bzzzzzzzzzzzzzzzz.

Little old mouse,
Little old mouse,
Where have you been?
I've been all through the house,
Said little old mouse.
Squeak-eak-eak-eak-eak.

—Margaret Wise Brown

The Caterpillar

Brown and furry
Caterpillar in a hurry;
Take your walk
To the shady leaf or stalk.

May no toad spy you,
May the little birds pass by you;
Spin and die,
To live again a butterfly.

—Christina G. Rossetti

14

Sally and Manda

Sally and Manda are two little lizards
Who gobble up flies in their two little gizzards.
They live by a toadstool near two little hummocks
And crawl all around on their two little stomachs.

—Alice B. Campbell

The Little Turtle

There was a little turtle.
He lived in a box.
He swam in a puddle.
He climbed on the rocks.

He snapped at a mosquito.
He snapped at a flea.
He snapped at a minnow.
And he snapped at me.

He caught the mosquito.
He caught the flea.
He caught the minnow.
But he didn't catch me.

—Vachel Lindsay

15

Drippy Weather

Geese keep dry
in drippy weather,
oiling feather after feather.

I keep just as dry
. . . and quicker.
I just have to wear my slicker.

—Aileen Fisher

Rain

The rain is raining all around,
It falls on field and tree,
It rains on the umbrellas here,
And on the ships at sea.

—Robert Louis Stevenson

Trains

Over the mountains,
Over the plains,
Over the rivers,
Here come the trains.

Carrying passengers,
Carrying mail,
Bringing their precious loads
In without fail.

Thousands of freight cars
All rushing on
Through day and darkness,
Through dusk and dawn.

Over the mountains,
Over the plains,
Over the rivers,
Here come the trains.

—James S. Tippett

Spring Rain

The storm came up so very quick
   It couldn't have been quicker.
I should have brought my hat along,
   I should have brought my slicker.

My hair is wet, my feet are wet,
   I couldn't be much wetter.
I fell into a river once,
   But this is even better.

—Marchette Chute

Reflection

In the mirror
I can see
Lots of things
But mostly—me.

—Myra Cohn Livingston

High-Heeled Shoes

I like to wear my Mommie's shoes.
I mean the pairs she doesn't use.

I pick the ones with highest heels,
You can't imagine how it feels

To walk around, go out the door,
Clump-clumping all across the floor.

—Kate Cox Goddard

Drinking Fountain

When I climb up
   To get a drink,
It doesn't work
   The way you'd think.

I turn it up.
   The water goes
And hits me right
   Upon the nose.

I turn it down
   To make it small
And don't get any
   Drink at all.

      —Marchette Chute

Blum

Dog means dog,
And cat means cat;
And there are lots
Of words like that.

A cart's a cart
To pull or shove,
A plate's a plate
To eat off of.

But there are other
Words I say
When I am left
Alone to play.

Blum is one.
Blum is a word
That very few
Have ever heard.

I like to say it,
"Blum, Blum, Blum"—
I do it loud
Or in a hum.

      —Dorothy Aldis

Wild Beasts

I will be a lion
   And you shall be a bear,
And each of us will have a den
   Beneath a nursery chair;
And you must growl and growl and growl,
   And I will roar and roar,
And then—why, then—you'll growl again,
   And I will roar some more!

      —Evaleen Stein

My Dog

His nose is short and scrubby;
    His ears hang rather low;
And he always brings the stick back,
    No matter how far you throw.

Chums

He sits and begs; he gives a paw;
    He is, as you can see,
The finest dog you ever saw,
    And he belongs to me.

He follows everywhere I go
    And even when I swim.
I laugh because he thinks, you know,
    That I belong to him.

—Arthur Guiterman

He gets spanked rather often
    For things he shouldn't do,
Like lying-on-beds, and barking,
    And eating up shoes when they're new.

He always wants to be going
    Where he isn't supposed to go.
He tracks up the house when it's snowing—
    Oh, puppy, I love you so.

—Marchette Chute

20

A Swing Song

Swing, swing,
Sing, sing,
Here! my throne, and I am a king!
Swing, sing,
Swing, sing,
Farewell, earth, for I'm on the wing!

Low, high,
Here I fly,
Like a bird through sunny sky;
Free, free,
Over the lea,
Over the mountain, over the sea!

Up, down,
Up and down,
Which is the way to London Town?
Where? Where?
Up in the air,
Close your eyes and now you are there!

Soon, soon,
Afternoon,
Over the sunset, over the moon;
Far, far,
Over all bar,
Sweeping on from star to star!

No, no,
Low, low,
Sweeping daisies with my toe.
Slow, slow,
To and fro,
Slow—slow—slow—slow.

—William Allingham

The Swing

How do you like to go up in a swing,
Up in the air so blue?
Oh, I do think it the pleasantest thing
Ever a child can do!

Up in the air and over the wall,
Till I can see so wide,
Rivers and trees and cattle and all
Over the countryside—

Till I look down on the garden green,
Down on the roof so brown—
Up in the air I go flying again,
Up in the air and down!

—Robert Louis Stevenson

The Picnic

We brought a rug for sitting on,
Our lunch was in a box.
The sand was warm. We didn't wear
Hats or shoes or socks.

Waves came curling up the beach.
We waded. It was fun.
Our sandwiches were different kinds.
I dropped my jelly one.

—Dorothy Aldis

Day-Time Moon

In the morning when the sun
Is shining down on everyone
How strange to see a daytime moon
Floating like a pale balloon
Over house and barn and tree
Without one star for company.

—Dorothy Aldis

Yellow

Green is go,
and red is stop,
and yellow is peaches
with cream on top.

Earth is brown,
and blue is sky;
yellow looks well
on a butterfly.

Clouds are white,
black, pink, or mocha;
yellow's a dish of
tapioca.

—David McCord

I'm Glad

I'm glad the sky is painted blue,
And the earth is painted green,
With such a lot of nice fresh air
All sandwiched in between.

—Anonymous

23

Jump or Jiggle

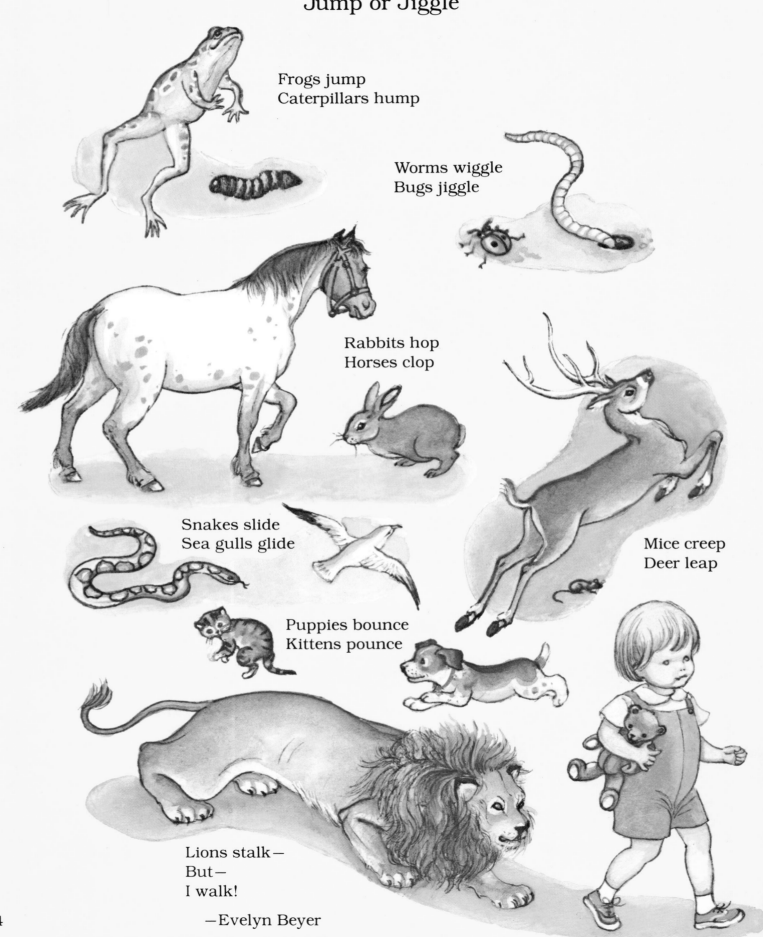

Frogs jump
Caterpillars hump

Worms wiggle
Bugs jiggle

Rabbits hop
Horses clop

Snakes slide
Sea gulls glide

Mice creep
Deer leap

Puppies bounce
Kittens pounce

Lions stalk—
But—
I walk!

—Evelyn Beyer

24

There Once Was a Puffin

Oh, there once was a Puffin
Just the shape of a muffin,
And he lived on an island
In the
    bright
       blue sea!

He ate little fishes,
That were most delicious,
And he had them for supper
And he
    had
       them
          for tea.

But this poor little Puffin,
He couldn't play nothin',
For he hadn't anybody
To
    play
       with
          at all.

So he sat on his island
And he cried for a while, and
He felt very lonely,
And he
    felt
       very small.

Then along came the fishes,
And they said, "If you wishes,
You can have us for playmates,
Instead
    of
       for
          tea!"

So they now play together,
In all sorts of weather,
And the Puffin eats pancakes,
Like you
    and
       like
          me.

—Florence Page Jaques

Who Has Seen the Wind

Who has seen the wind?
   Neither I nor you:
But when the leaves hang trembling
   The wind is passing through.

Who has seen the wind?
   Neither you nor I:
But when the trees bow down their heads
   The wind is passing by.

          —Christina G. Rossetti

Threats

I'll go away and never come back.
    Rickity-rack
    I'll never come back.
I'll put my clothes in a paper sack.
    Rickity-rack
    In a paper sack.

Away I'll go and never be seen.
    Stickity-lean
    And never be seen.
And they'll be sorry they were so mean.
    Stickity-lean
    That they were so mean.

"Oh, what a charming child," they'll say.
    Hippity-hay
    "Charming!" they'll say.
"But why did she go so far away?"
    Hippity-hay
    "So far away!"

"If she'd come back, we tell you true,"
    Whippity-woo
    "We tell you true,
"We'd do just what she wants us to."
    Whippity-woo
    "She wants us to."

But it will be too late for that.
    Bippity-bat
    Too late for that.
For I'll be gone in my best hat.
    Bippity-bat
    In my best hat.

    Rickity-wickity
    Lickity-splickity
    Rickity, rickity
        Rack

—Marci Ridlon

A Calendar

January brings the snow,
Makes our feet and fingers glow.

February brings the rain,
Thaws the frozen lake again.

March brings breezes, loud and shrill,
To stir the dancing daffodil.

April brings the primrose sweet,
Scatters daisies at our feet.

May brings flocks of pretty lambs
Skipping by their fleecy dams.

June brings tulips, lilies, roses,
Fills the children's hands with posies.

Hot July brings cooling showers,
Apricots, and gillyflowers.

August brings the sheaves of corn,
Then the harvest home is borne.

Warm September brings the fruit;
Sportsmen then begin to shoot.

Fresh October brings the pheasant;
Then to gather nuts is pleasant.

Dull November brings the blast;
Then the leaves are whirling fast.

Chill December brings the sleet,
Blazing fire, and Christmas treat.

—Sara Coleridge

The Snail

The snail doesn't know where he's going
and he doesn't especially care,
one place is as good as another
and here is no better than there.

The snail's unconcerned with direction
but happily goes on his way
in search of specifically nothing
at two or three inches a day.

—Jack Prelutsky

Mice

I think mice
Are rather nice.
 Their tails are long,
 Their faces small,
 They haven't any
 Chins at all.
 Their ears are pink,
 Their teeth are white,
 They run about
 The house at night.
 They nibble things
 They shouldn't touch
 And no one seems
 To like them much
But I think mice
Are nice.

—Rose Fyleman

Fish

Fish have fins
and fish have tails;
fish have skins
concealed by scales.
Fish are seldom
found on land;
fish would rather
swim than stand.

— Jack Prelutsky

Hide and Seek

When I am alone, and quite alone,
I play a game, and it's all my own.

I hide myself
Behind myself,
And then I try
To find myself.

I hide in the closet,
Where no one can see;
Then I start looking
Around for me.

I hide myself
And look for myself;
There once was a shadow
I took for myself.

I hide in a corner;
I hide in the bed;
And when I come near me
I pull in my head!

— A. B. Shiffrin

Near and Far

Little children far away,
'Cross the ocean wide,
'Though they do not look like us
Are the same inside.

Other children everywhere
I would like to meet,
Ones who live across the sea
Others down the street.

— Kate Cox Goddard

The Airplane

No eagle flies through sun and rain
So swiftly as an airplane.
I wish she would come swooping down
Between the steeples of the town
And lift me right up off my feet
And take me high above the street,
That all the other boys might see
The little speck that would be me.

—Rowena Bastin Bennett

Skyscrapers

Do skyscrapers ever grow tired
Of holding themselves up high?
Do they ever shiver on frosty nights
With their tops against the sky?
Do they feel lonely sometimes
Because they have grown so tall?
Do they ever wish they could lie right down
And never get up at all?

—Rachel Lyman Field

E

E is the Escalator
   That gives an elegant ride.
You step on the stair
With an easy air
   And up and up you glide.
It's nicer than scaling ladders
   Or scrambling 'round a hill,
For you climb and climb
But all the time
   You're really standing still.

—Phyllis McGinley

Furry Bear

If I were a bear,
   And a big bear too,
I shouldn't much care
   If it froze or snew;
I shouldn't much mind
   If it snowed or friz—
I'd be all fur-lined
   With a coat like his!

For I'd have fur boots and a brown fur wrap.
And brown fur knickers and a big fur cap.
I'd have a fur muffle-ruff to cover my jaws,
And brown fur mittens on my big brown paws.
With a big brown furry-down up to my head,
I'd sleep all the winter in a big fur bed.

—A. A. Milne

33

New Shoes

When I am walking down the street
I do so like to watch my feet.
Perhaps you do not know the news,
Mother has bought me fine new shoes!

—Marjorie Seymour Watts

34

At the Zoo

There are lions and roaring tigers, and enormous camels and things,
There are biffalo-buffalo-bisons, and a great big bear with wings,
There's a sort of a tiny potamus, and a tiny nosserus too—
But *I* gave buns to the elephant when *I* went down to the Zoo!

There are badgers and bidgers and bodgers, and a Super-intendent's House
There are masses of goats, and a Polar, and different kinds of mouse,
And I think there's a sort of a something which is called a wallaboo—
But *I* gave buns to the elephant when *I* went down to the Zoo!

If you try to talk to the bison, he never quite understands;
You can't shake hands with a mingo—he doesn't like shaking hands.
And lions and roaring tigers *hate* saying, "How do you do?"—
But *I* give buns to the elephant when *I* go down to the Zoo!

—A. A. Milne   35

Christmas

My goodness, my goodness,
It's Christmas again.
The bells are all ringing.
I do not know when
I've been so excited.
The tree is all fixed,
The candles are lighted,
The pudding is mixed.
The wreath's on the door
And the carols are sung.
The presents are wrapped
And the holly is hung.
The turkey is sitting
All safe in its pan,
And I am behaving
As calm as I can.

—Marchette Chute

A Sledding Song

Sing a song of winter,
  Of frosty clouds in air!
Sing a song of snowflakes
  Falling everywhere.

Sing a song of winter!
  Sing a song of sleds!
Sing a song of tumbling
  Over heels and heads.

Up and down a hillside
  When the moon is bright,
Sledding is a tiptop
  Wintertime delight.

—Norman C. Schlichter

A New Friend

They've taken in the furniture;
I watched them carefully.
I wondered, "Will there be a child
Just right to play with me?"

So I peeked through the garden fence
(I couldn't wait to see).
I found the little boy next door
Was peeking back at me.

—Marjorie Allen Anderson

38

Animal Crackers

Animal crackers, and cocoa to drink,
That is the finest of suppers, I think;
When I'm grown up and can have what I please
I think I shall always insist upon these.

What do *you* choose when you're offered a treat?
When Mother says, "What would you like best to eat?"
Is it waffles and syrup, or cinnamon toast?
It's cocoa and animals that *I* love the most!

—Christopher Morley

Mix a Pancake

Mix a pancake,
Stir a pancake,
    Pop it in the pan;
Fry the pancake,
Toss the pancake—
    Catch it if you can.

—Christina G. Rossetti

Table Manners

The Goops they lick their fingers,
    The Goops they lick their knives,
They spill their broth on the table-cloth;
    They live untidy lives.
The Goops they talk while eating,
    And loud and fast they chew,
So that is why I am glad that I
    Am not a Goop. Are you?

—Gelett Burgess

Go To Bed First

Go to bed first,
A golden purse;
Go to bed second,
A golden pheasant;
Go to bed third,
A golden bird.

—Anonymous

Woolly Blanket

I have a woolly blanket.
It's cuddly and it's pink.
And it is very dear to me,
More so than you would think.

Whenever I go traveling,
That blanket travels, too.
And if I should forget it, why
I don't know what I'd do.

It always goes to bed with me,
I like to feel it near,
Because it is so cuddly and
So very, very dear.

—Kate Cox Goddard

Bedtime

Five minutes, five minutes more, please!
    Let me stay five minutes more!
Can't I just finish the castle
    I'm building here on the floor?
Can't I just finish the story
    I'm reading here in my book?
Can't I just finish this bead-chain—
    It *almost* is finished, look!
Can't I just finish this game, please?
    When a game's once begun
It's a pity never to find out
    Whether you've lost or won.
Can't I just stay five minutes?
    Well, can't I stay just four?
Three minutes, then? two minutes?
    Can't I stay one minute more?

—Eleanor Farjeon

Before the Bath

It's cold, cold, cold,
And the water shines wet,
And the longer I wait
The colder I get.

I can't quite make
Myself hop in
All shivery-cold
In just my skin.

Yet the water's warm
In the tub, I know.
So—one, two, three,
And IN I go!

—Corinna Marsh

After a Bath

After my bath
I try, try, try
to wipe myself
till I'm dry, dry, dry.

Hands to wipe
and fingers and toes
and two wet legs
and a shiny nose.

Just think how much
less time I'd take
if I were a dog
and could shake, shake, shake.

—Aileen Fisher

City

In the morning the city
Spreads its wings
Making a song
In stone that sings.

In the evening the city
Goes to bed
Hanging lights
About its head.

—Langston Hughes

Good Night

This day's done.
Tomorrow's another.

Good night, Daddy.
Good night, Mother.

Good night, kitten,
book, and brother . . .

In one dream
and out the other.

—Aileen Fisher

The Star

Twinkle, twinkle, little star,
How I wonder what you are!
Up above the world, so high,
Like a diamond in the sky.

—Ann and Jane Taylor

Firefly

A little light is going by,
Is going up to see the sky,
A little light with wings.

I never could have thought of it,
To have a little bug all lit
And made to go on wings.

—Elizabeth Madox Roberts

Goodnight, Little People

The evening is coming
   The sun sinks to rest,
The rooks are all flying
   Straight home to the nest.
"Caw!" says the rook, as he flies overhead.
"It's time little people were going to bed."

The flowers are closing;
   The daisy's asleep,
The primrose is buried
   In slumber so deep.
Shut up for the night is the pimpernel red;
It's time little people were going to bed!
   Good night, little people,
      Good night and good night;
   Sweet dreams to your eyelids
      Till dawning of light.
The evening has come, there's no more to be said;
It's time little people were going to bed!

—Thomas Hood

Stars

Bright stars, light stars,
Shining-in-the-night stars,
Little twinkly, winkly stars,
Deep in the sky.

Yellow stars, red stars,
Shine-when-I'm-in-bed stars,
Oh how many blinky stars,
Far, far away!

—Rhoda W. Bacmeister

Index of First Lines

Acknowledgments

The publishers have made every effort to locate the owners of all copyrighted material and to obtain permission to reprint the following poems. Any errors are unintentional, and corrections will be made in future editions if necessary.

Addison-Wesley Publishing Company, Inc., for "The Rabbit Skip." Reprinted from NIBBLE. NIBBLE. © 1959, by Margaret Wise Brown, by permission of Addison-Wesley Publishing Company, Inc.   Branden Press Incorporated for "New Shoes" by Marjorie Seymour Watts.   Curtis Brown, Ltd. for "E." Reprinted by permission of Curtis Brown, Ltd. Copyright 1948 by Phyllis McGinley, copyright renewed © 1976 by Phyllis McGinley.   Marchette Chute for "Christmas," "Drinking Fountain," and "Spring Rain," from RHYMES ABOUT THE CITY by Marchette Chute. Copyright 1946 (Macmillan), renewal 1974 by Marchette Chute. Reprinted by permission of the author. For "My Dog" from RHYMES ABOUT OURSELVES by Marchette Chute. Copyright 1932 (Macmillan), renewal 1960 by Marchette Chute. Reprinted by permission of the author.   Thomas Y. Crowell, Publishers, for "Good Night." From IN ONE DOOR AND OUT THE OTHER: A BOOK OF POEMS BY AILEEN FISHER. Copyright © 1969 by Aileen Fisher. By permission of Thomas Y. Crowell, Publishers.   Dodd, Mead & Company, Inc., and The Society of Authors as the literary representative of the Estate of Rose Fyleman for "The Birthday Child." Reprinted by permission of Dodd, Mead & Company, Inc., from ROUND THE MULBERRY BUSH by Rose Fyleman. Copyright 1928 by Dodd, Mead & Company, Inc. Copyright renewed 1955 by Rose Fyleman.   Doubleday and Company, Inc., and The Society of Authors as the literary representative of the Estate of Rose Fyleman for "Mice" from FIFTY-ONE NEW NURSERY RHYMES by Josette Frank. Copyright 1931, 1932 by Doubleday & Company, Inc. Reprinted by permission of the publisher. For "Singing Time" from THE FAIRY GREEN by Rose Fyleman. Copyright 1923 by George H. Doran Company. Reprinted by permission of Doubleday & Company, Inc.   Dover Publications, for "Table Manners" from GOOPS AND HOW TO BE THEM by Gelett Burgess, Dover Publications, New York, 1968.   Elsevier-Dutton Publishing Co., Inc., for "Stars" from STORIES TO BEGIN ON by Rhoda W. Bacmeister. Copyright 1940 by E. P. Dutton & Co., Inc. Renewal © 1968 by Rhoda W. Bacmeister. For "Jump or Jiggle" by Evelyn Beyer and "Little Black Bug" by Margaret Wise Brown from ANOTHER HERE AND NOW STORYBOOK by Lucy Sprague Mitchell. Copyright, 1937, by E.P. Dutton & Co., Inc. Renewal, 1965, by Lucy Sprague Mitchell. Reprinted by permission of the publisher, E.P. Dutton.   Elsevier-Dutton Publishing Co., Inc., and McClelland & Stewart Ltd. for "At the Zoo" and "Puppy and I" from WHEN WE WERE VERY YOUNG by A. A. Milne. Copyright, 1924, by E. P. Dutton & Co., Inc. Renewal 1952 by A. A. Milne. For "Furry Bear" from NOW WE ARE SIX by A. A. Milne. Copyright, 1927, by E.P. Dutton & Co., Inc. Renewal, 1955, by A. A. Milne. Reprinted by permission of the publisher, E.P. Dutton.   Aileen Fisher for "After a Bath" and "Bird Talk" from UP THE WINDY HILL, Abelard, N.Y., 1953. Copyright renewed 1981. By permission of the author.   Follet Publishing Company for "The Airplane" from SONGS FROM AROUND A TOADSTOOL TABLE by Rowena Bastin Bennet. Copyright 1930 by Follet Publishing Company. Used by permission of Follet Publishing Company.   Grosset & Dunlap, Inc., Publishers, for "High-Heeled Shoes," "Near and Far," and "Woolly Blanket" from POEMS FOR LITTLE EARS by Kate Cox Goddard, copyright 1939, 1944, 1962 by Platt & Munk Co., reprinted by permission of Grosset & Dunlap, Inc.

Harcourt Brace Jovanovich, Inc., for "Reflection." From WIDE AWAKE AND OTHER POEMS. © 1959 by Myra Cohn Livingston. Reprinted by permission of Harcourt Brace Jovanovich, Inc.   Harper & Row, Publishers, Inc., for "Five Years Old," from A POCKETFUL OF POEMS by Marie Louise Allen. Text copyright © 1957 by Marie Allen Howarth. For "Trains" from CRICKETY CRICKET! THE BEST-LOVED POEMS OF JAMES S. TIPPETT. Poem Copyright, 1929, by Harper & Row, Publishers, Inc. Renewed 1957 by James S. Tippett. By permission of Harper & Row, Publishers, Inc.   Highlights for Children, Inc., for "A New Friend" by Marjorie Allen Anderson, Children's Activities, June 1950, Copyright Children's Activities. Used by permission of Highlights for Children, Inc., Columbus, Ohio.   J. B. Lippincott, Publishers, for "Bedtime" from ELEANOR FARJEON'S POEMS FOR CHILDREN. Poem Copyright, 1933, 1961, by Eleanor Farjeon. By permission of J. B. Lippincott, Publishers.   Little, Brown, and Company for "Yellow" from AWAY AND AGO. Copyright © 1974 by David McCord. By permission of Little, Brown, and Company.   Macmillan Publishing Co., Inc., for "Skyscrapers." Reprinted with permission of Macmillan Publishing Co., Inc., from POEMS by Rachel Field (New York: Macmillan, 1957). For "The Little Turtle." Reprinted with permission of Macmillan Publishing Company from COLLECTED POEMS by Vachel Lindsay. Copyright 1920 by Macmillan Publishing Co., Inc., renewed 1948 by Elizabeth C. Lindsay.   The Literary Trustees of Walter de la Mare and The Society of Authors as their representative for "Some One" by Walter de la Mare.   The Estate of Christopher Morley for the first eight lines of "Animal Crackers" from SONGS FOR A LITTLE HOUSE. Copyright 1917, renewed 1945 by Christopher Morley.   Harold Ober Associates Incorporated for "City" by Langston Hughes. Reprinted by permission of Harold Ober Associates Incorporated. Copyright © 1958 by Langston Hughes.   Pantheon Books, Inc., for "Field Mouse to Kitchen Mouse," from MOUSE CHORUS, by Elizabeth Coatsworth. Copyright © 1955 by Pantheon Books, Inc. Reprinted by permission of Pantheon Books, a Division of Random House, Inc.   Jack Prelutsky for "Fish" and "The Snail." Copyright © 1967, 1970 by Jack Prelutsky.   Putnam Publishing Group for "Blum," "Day-Time Moon," and "The Picnic." Reprinted by permission of G.P. Putnam's Sons from HOP. SKIP. & JUMP by Dorothy Aldis. Copyright 1934, renewed © 1961 by Dorothy Aldis.   Rand McNally & Company for "Sally and Manda," by Alice B. Campbell. From *Child Life Magazine*, copyright 1934, 1962 by Rand McNally & Company. For "There Once Was a Puffin" by Florence Page Jaques, from *Child Life Magazine*. Copyright 1930, 1958 by Rand McNally & Company. For "Mr. Rabbit" by Dixie Willson with permission of Dana W. Briggs, from *Child Life Magazine*, copyright 1924, 1952 by Rand McNally & Company.   David Ross for "Good-Morning" by Muriel Sipe.   Marci Ridlon for "Threats" from THAT WAS SUMMER. © 1969 by Marci Ridlon. Used with permission of the author.   Norman C. Schlichter for "A Sledding Song."   Louise H. Sclove for "Chums" by Arthur Guiterman from THE LAUGHING MUSE. Reprinted by permission of Louise H. Sclove.   A. B. Shiffrin for "Hide and Seek."   The University Society, Inc., for "Before a Bath" by Corinna Marsh.   Viking Penguin Inc., for "Firefly" from UNDER THE TREE by Elizabeth Madox Roberts. Copyright 1922 by B. W. Huebsch, Inc., copyright renewed 1950 by Ivor S. Roberts. Reprinted by permission of Viking Penguin Inc.   Xerox Corporation for "Drippy Weather" by Aileen Fisher. Special permission granted by *Weekly Reader*, published by Xerox Education Publications © Xerox Corporation.